Sport and My Body

Gymnastics

Catherine Veitch

www.raintreepublishers.co.uk
Visit our website to find out more information about Raintree books.

To order:
☎ Phone +44 (0) 1865 888066
🖹 Fax +44 (0) 1865 314091
🖥 Visit www.raintreepublishers.co.uk

Raintree is an imprint of Capstone Global Library Limited, a company incorporated in England and Wales having its registered office at 7 Pilgrim Street, London, EC4V 6LB – Registered company number: 6695582

Text © Capstone Global Library Limited 2009
First published in hardback in 2009
First published in paperback in 2010
The moral rights of the proprietor have been asserted.

Edited by Siân Smith, Rebecca Rissman, and Charlotte Guillain
Designed by Joanna Hinton-Malivoire
Picture research by Ruth Blair
Production by Duncan Gilbert
Originated by Chroma Graphics (Overseas) Pte. Ltd
Printed in China

ISBN 978 1 406 21111 5 (hardback)
13 12 11 10 09
10 9 8 7 6 5 4 3 2 1

ISBN 978 1 406 21117 7 (paperback)
14 13 12
10 9 8 7 6 5 4 3 2

British Library Cataloguing in Publication Data
Veitch, Catherine.
   Gymnastics. -- (Sport and my body)
   1. Gymnastics--Physiological aspects--Juvenile literature.
   2. Gymnastics--Social aspects--Juvenile literature.
   I. Title II. Series
   613.7'14-dc22

Acknowledgements
We would like to thank the following for permission to reproduce photographs: © Capstone Global Library Ltd p.**22** (Trevor Clifford); Corbis pp.**7** (Strauss/Curtis), **9** (Kevin Dodge), **10** (Anna Peisl/zefa), **12** (image100), **14** (Fancy/Veer), **16** (Adriane Moll/zefa), **23** (Kevin Dodge); Getty Images pp.**4** (Alistair Berg), **5**, **23** (Clive Brunskill), **6**, **23** (Frederick J. Brown/AFP), **13** (Susanna Price/DK), **17** (J. Clarke), **19** (Ableimages/Riser), **20** (Victoria Blackie/Photographer's Choice); Photolibrary pp.**8**, **23** (GoGo Images), **15**, **23** (Westend61), **18** (Big Cheese); Shutterstock pp.**11** (© Jiang Dao Hua), **21** (© Monkey Business Images).
Cover photograph of girls doing floor exercises reproduced with permission of Corbis/Anna Peisl/zefa. Back cover images reproduced with permission of Corbis: 1. child stretching (© Kevin Dodge); 2. child in a gym, bending backwards (© image100).

Every effort has been made to contact copyright holders of material reproduced in this book. Any omissions will be rectified in subsequent printings if notice is given to the publishers.

Contents

What is gymnastics?. 4

How do I learn gymnastics? 6

How do I use my arms and hands?. . . .8

How do I use my legs and feet? 10

How do I use the rest of my body?. . . 12

What happens to my body when
      I do gymnastics?. 14

How does it feel to do gymnastics? . . 16

How do I stay safe doing gymnastics? 18

Does gymnastics make me healthy?. . 20

Gymnastics equipment 22

Glossary 23

Index. 24

Find out more. 24

Some words are shown in bold, **like this**. You can find them in the glossary on page 23.

What is gymnastics?

Gymnastics is a type of exercise.
You can do jumps, rolls, and **balances**
in gymnastics.

You can do gymnastics on the floor or on **apparatus**.

How do I learn gymnastics?

You need an adult to teach you gymnastics. A teacher at your school or a gymnastics **coach** could teach you in a gym.

You need to be strong to do gymnastics. At first a teacher may help you learn to **balance**.

How do I use my arms and hands?

You use your arms to swing yourself under a bar. You use your hands to grip the bar tightly so you do not fall off.

You can stretch out your arms to help you **balance** on a beam. You can also make different shapes with your hands and arms.

How do I use my legs and feet?

You use your legs to do the splits. You should stretch your legs and point your toes in the splits.

You use your legs when you land after a jump. You should bend your knees when you land.

How do I use the rest of my body?

You can bend your back to make a bridge. This makes an arch shape with your body.

You can tuck yourself into a ball and roll backwards or forwards on a mat.

What other ways can you roll?

What happens to my body when I do gymnastics?

When you do gymnastics you will start to feel warm and sweaty. You will also feel out of breath.

muscle

Your heart will beat faster. The **muscles** in your arms and legs might ache and feel tired.

15

How does it feel to do gymnastics?

Gymnastics is a good way to have fun. You might make new friends as you do gymnastics together.

It feels good to get better at
gymnastics. As you get stronger
you can learn more **skills**.

How do I stay safe doing gymnastics?

You should always warm up before you do gymnastics. Stretching your **muscles** warms them up and stops you getting hurt.

It is important to listen to your **coach**. When you use the **apparatus** make sure nobody is in the way. Also, make sure you always use safety mats.

Does gymnastics make me healthy?

Gymnastics is good exercise and will help you keep fit. You should also eat healthy food and drink plenty of water.

To stay healthy you need to get plenty of rest, too. Then you can have fun doing lots of other exercise.

Gymnastics equipment

beam

mat

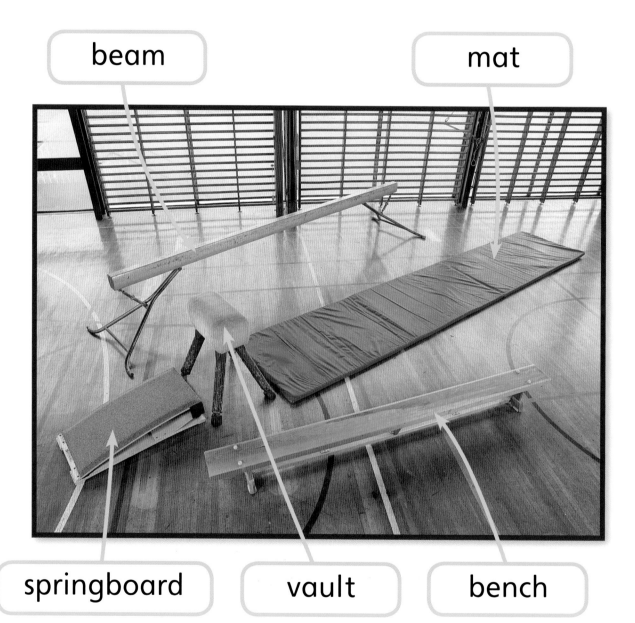

springboard

vault

bench

Glossary

 **apparatus** equipment. People often use large apparatus in gymnastics, such as beams to balance on. See page 22 for some examples of different apparatus.

 **balance** to keep yourself or an object steady so that it does not fall

 **coach** trainer. A coach helps people to learn and become better at something.

 **muscle** part of your body that helps you to move. Exercise can make muscles bigger and stronger.

 **skill** ability to do something well. You can develop different skills through training and practice.

Index

apparatus 5, 19, 23

balance 4, 7, 9, 23

beam 9, 22, 23

coach 6, 19, 23

equipment 22, 23

jump 4, 11

learn 6, 7, 17, 23

mat 13, 19, 22

muscle 15, 18, 23

roll 4, 13

safety 18, 19

skill 17, 23

splits 10

stretch 9, 10, 18

Find out more

http://www.playsportstv.com/box.php?id=13&media-id=210
On this site, you will find some great warm-up exercises to do.

http://kids.nationalgeographic.co.uk/Games/ActionGames/
Geogames-monkey-bars-gymnastics
Play the Monkey Bar game to learn about gymnastics!